The Path
Less Taken

July 1999

To Anne

With love and
prayers from

Pauline x

For my family,
friends and teachers,
and for all those on the journey,
especially my mother, Josephine,
who, in her eighties,
holds high the lantern.

Most of the scripture verses are taken from the
New International Version, however for the sake of poetry, some passages
are taken from the King James, Revised Standard, Living Bible,
New American and the New American Standard.

Published by C.R. Gibson,® Norwalk, Connecticut 06856
C.R. Gibson® is a registered trademark of Thomas Nelson, Inc.
Printed in the United States of America
ISBN-0-7667-0386-X
GB2007

The Path
Less Taken

WORDS TO GUIDE YOU

By JoAnna O'Keefe
Illustrated by Sharon Engel

C.R. Gibson®
Norwalk, Connecticut 06856

Introduction

I wrote, "The Path Less Taken," at a time in my life when I was at a crossroads. I wanted to change direction, but I was afraid. One night, I sat before an open fire in the familyroom of our farmhouse contemplating my journey.

I was tired and felt like giving up. Yet a voice within kept urging me to follow my heart. For a long while I sat in silence wanting to draw close to God, wanting guidance.

Around dawn I picked up my journal, and in pale flickering light, filled the blank white pages with

my fears, my hopes, and my dreams. I wrote,
I cried, and I prayed until a gentle peace came
over my spirit. Still I was unsure.

Then one glorious morning, walking in the
woods with my dogs, I heard a still voice, like
a whisper in the wind, "Trust in me, my child,
by my Spirit you'll be led."

It is my hope that the meditations in this simple
book will help you to trust, and lead you to a
quiet place within, where God speaks in a
whisper and gives courage to the soul to take
another path.

— JoAnna O'Keefe

Lord,

I need guidance

Which path should I take?

I stand at the crossroads,

Fearing a mistake.

Show me the path
where I should go,
O Lord, point out the
right road for me to walk.

Psalms 25:4

Help me to do your will,
for you are my God.

Psalms 143:10

Send forth your light
and your truth,
let them guide me . . .

Psalms 43:3

I call on you, O God,
for you will answer me;
give ear to me and hear my prayer.

Psalms 17:6

want to change direction

From the well-worn path I know,

And follow the one less traveled,

But I'm afraid to go.

Lord, when doubt fills my mind
when my heart is in turmoil,
quiet me and give me renewed hope and cheer.

Psalms 94:19

*You have seen me tossing
and turning in the night.*

Psalms 56:8

*My thoughts trouble me
and I am distraught.*

Psalms 55:2

Yet

I hear you calling,

In the quiet of the night,

Urging me to go,

Trusting in your light.

My soul yearns for you in the night;
in the morning my spirit longs for you.

Psalms 26:9

I can never be lost to your Spirit!

Psalms 139:7

*You, O Lord, keep my lamp burning
my God turns darkness into light.*

Psalms 18:28

*If I rise on the wings of the dawn,
if I settle on the far side of the sea,
even there your hand will hold me fast.*

Psalms 139:9-10

know your word should be

A lamp unto my feet,

And you will light my path

And give me bread to eat.

O Lord God, You are God
and your words are truth.

Samuel 7:28

*Even the darkness will not be dark
to you: the night will shine like the
day, for darkness is as light to you.*

Psalms 139:12

*I am a wayfarer of earth
hide not your commands from me.*

Psalms 119:19

*Make me understand...
for then I shall see your miracles.*

Psalms 119:27

trust you, Lord,

I know you'll shepherd me.

Still I feel uncertain,

I want security.

You have searched me and know me.
You know when I sit and when I rise;
you perceive my thoughts from afar.

Psalms 139:3

Don't fail me Lord, for I am
trusting you.

Psalms 25:2

Your love,
O Lord, endures forever . . .
do not abandon the works of your hands.

Psalms 138:8

Protect me as you would the pupil
of your eye; hide me in the shadow
of your wings.

Psalms 17:8

*I'm*

afraid!

Afraid I'll fail or fall,

Afraid I'll lose my way.

Still, I hear you call.

When I am afraid
I will put my trust in Thee.

Psalms 56:3

God did not give me a spirit of timidity,
but a spirit of power, of love and of self-discipline.

2 Timothy 1:7

I give no thought to what lies behind
but push on to what is ahead.

Philippians 3:13

Let the morning bring me word
of your unfailing love, for I have
put my trust in you.

Psalms 143:8

Trust

in me my child,

With both your heart and head;

Take a step in faith,

By my Spirit you'll be led.

Don't be afraid...
I have called you by name;
you are mine.

Isaiah 43:1

Behold,
I am with you.

Genesis 28:15

Stand at the crossroads and look;
ask for the ancient paths,
and where the good way is, and walk in it,
and you will find rest for your soul.

Jeremiah 6:16

The Spirit of truth will guide you.

John 16:13

Do

not fear the darkness,

By still waters you'll find rest,

The journey of your soul

Will be a life long quest.

Let not your heart be troubled,
neither let it be afraid.

John 14:27

Come with me to a
quiet place and rest.

Mark 6:31

I will turn the darkness into light
and make the rough places smooth.

Isaiah 42:16

There is a time for everything
and a season for every
activity under heaven.

Ecclesiastes 3:1

Take

the path less traveled;

Your heart will find the way.

I will give you Light—

Just have faith, and pray.

*Be joyful in hope, patient in affliction,
faithful in prayer.*

Romans 12:12

Whatever is true, whatever is noble,
whatever is right, whatever is pure,
whatever is lovely, whatever is admirable—
if anything is excellent or praiseworthy—
think about such things.

Philippians 4:8

Be strong, and let your heart take courage.

Psalms 31:24

I am the way the truth and the light.

John 14:6

Put

your trust in me,

I'll not abandon you.

I will give you strength

To see the journey through.

Trust in me with all your heart
and lean not on your own understanding

Proverbs 3:5

*Faith is the assurance of things
hoped for, the conviction
of things not seen.*

Hebrews 11:1

*Be watchful, stand firm in your
faith, be courageous, be strong.
Let all that you do be done in love.*

1 Corinthians 16:13

*When you go through deep waters...
I will be with you.*

Isaiah 43:2

Come

away each day

In quiet prayer with me.

I will give you courage

And set your spirit free.

Be still, and know that I am God.

Psalms 46:10

Be not conformed to this world:
but be transformed by
the renewing of your mind.

Romans 12:2

In quietness and in trust
shall be your strength

Isaiah 40:31

A new heart I will give you,
and a new spirit
I will put within you.

Ezekiel 36:26

will bear you up;

On eagle's wings you'll soar.

A faithful heart in prayer

I never will ignore.

*Those who hope in the Lord
will renew their strength. They will
soar on wings like eagles; they will
run and not be faint.*

Isaiah 40:31

Be not afraid, only believe.

Mark 5:36

*If you have faith as small as a
mustard seed...Nothing will be
impossible for you.*

Matthew 17:20

*I have told you these things, so that
in me you may have peace.*

John 16:33

The Path

Lord, I need guidance
Which path should I take?
I stand at the crossroads,
Fearing a mistake.

I want to change direction
From the well-worn path I know,
And follow the one less traveled,
But I'm afraid to go.

Yet I hear you calling,
In the quiet of the night,
Urging me to go,
Trusting in your light.

I know your word should be
A lamp unto my feet,
And you will light my path
And give me bread to eat.

I trust you, Lord
I know you'll shepherd me.
Still I feel uncertain,
I want security.

I'm afraid!
Afraid I'll fail or fall,
Afraid I'll lose my way.
Still, I hear you call.

Less Taken

Trust in me my child,
With both your heart and head;
Take a step in faith,
By my Spirit you'll be led.

Do not fear the darkness,
By still waters you'll find rest,
The journey of your soul
Will be a life long quest.

Take the path less traveled;
Your heart will find the way.
I will give you Light—
Just have faith, and pray.

Put your trust in me,
I'll not abandon you.
I will give you strength
To see the journey through.

Come away each day
In quiet prayer with me.
I will give you courage
And set your spirit free.

I will bear you up;
On eagle's wings you'll soar.
A faithful heart in prayer
I never will ignore.

— JoAnna O'Keefe

Colophon
Editor: Eileen D'Andrea
Graphic Designer: Aurora Campanella
Typesetting: Millicent Iacono

Type set in Shelley Allegro Script
Garamond Book and Simoncini Garamond Italic